Odd Jobs and Even Stevens

Teacher instructions Su 1, 2
Colour the shirts of the Odd Jobs team green, and the shirts of the Even Stevens team, blue. Write the numbers for each team on their banners in order.

Date ____________

Steps of 5s and 3s

Teacher instructions Su 1, 3

Complete the number sequences by counting on in steps of fives and threes.

Collins Primary Maths

Number Workbook 3

Name ____________________

COLLINS

Date ____________

Quilt counting

Teacher instructions Su 1, 1

In each row of the patchwork quilt count on in 2s and fill in the missing numbers.

 Date ______________

Tenmorethan Town

Teacher instructions Su 2, 1

Match each person's clothes to the colour of their house. Look at the number on their clothes. Write the number that is 10 more on their house.

Date ________________

More or less balloons

Teacher instructions Su 2, 2

In each set colour the balloon showing more in yellow, and the balloon showing less in red. On the middle balloon write a number that lies between them.

Date ____________

Countryside counting

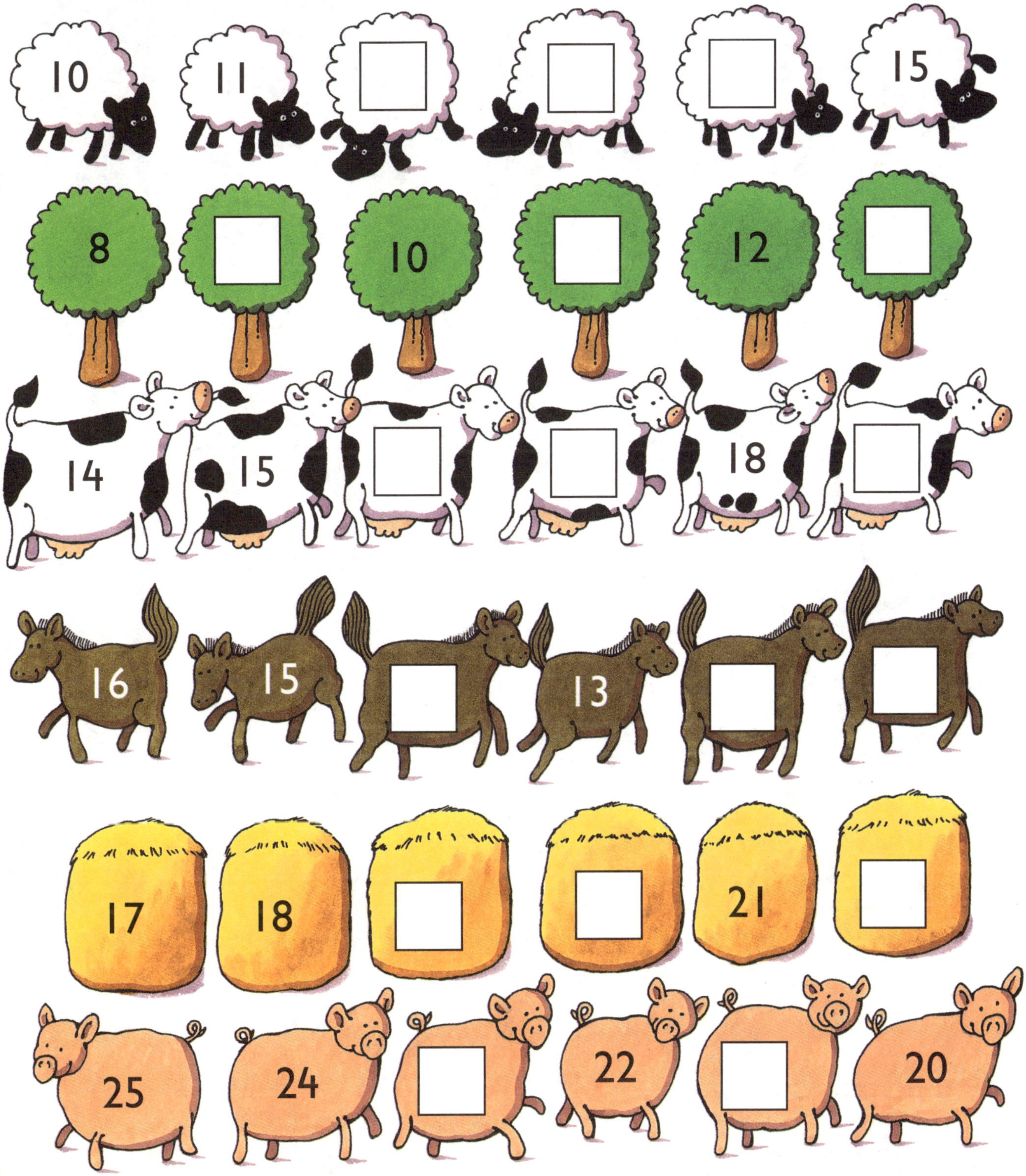

Date ______________

Ball pond addition

6 + 1 + 3 = 10

○ + ○ + ○ = 13

○ + ○ + ○ = 7

○ + ○ + ○ = 11

○ + ○ + ○ = 12

○ + ○ + ○ = 16

Teacher instructions Su 2, 4

Look at the picture. Then in each row find three numbers that, when added together, make the total in the box. Write the numbers on the balls.

Date ____________

Playground addition

Teacher instructions Su 2, 5

Add the numbers on each child's shirt. Match the total to a number on the playground equipment and colour the shirt in a matching colour.

Date ____________

Bridging through 10 sails

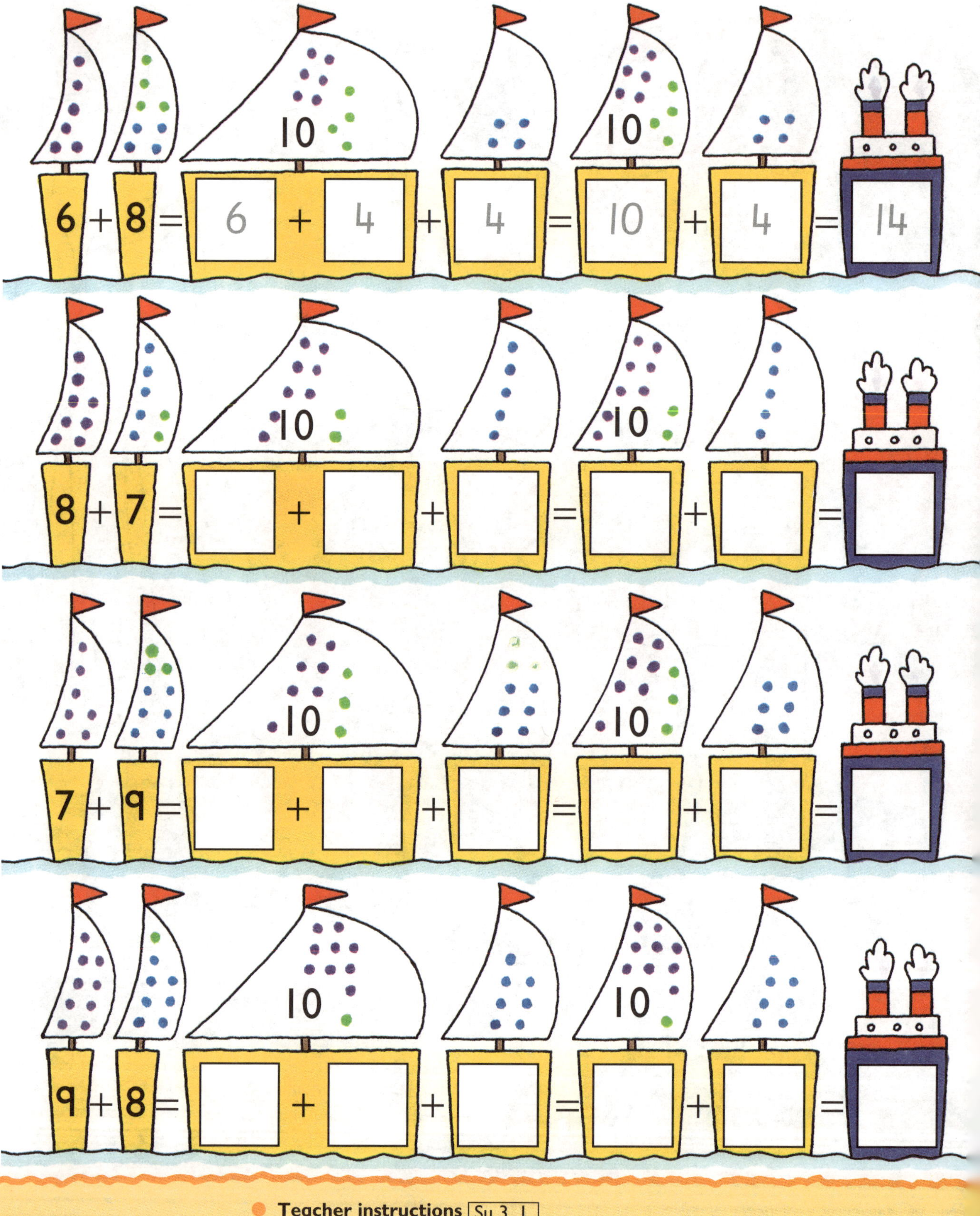

Teacher instructions Su 3, 1

Look at the different-coloured dots on the sails. Write the number bond for each addition problem. Then complete the sequence and write the total on the ship.

Date ____________

Patterns of nine

Teacher instructions Su 3, 2

In each row of windows solve the addition and subtraction problems which make 9 by writing in the correct number.

Date ________

Space rocket addition

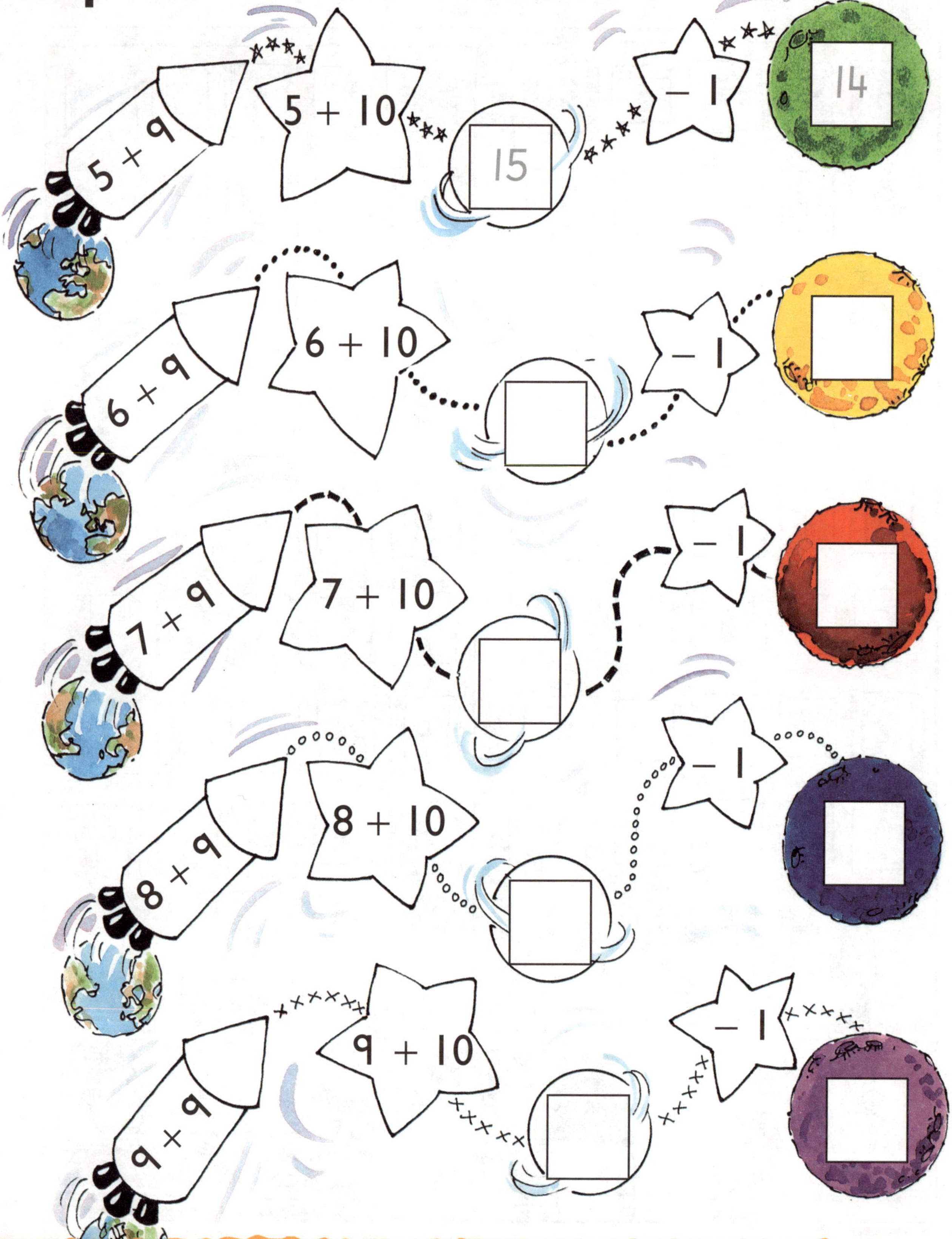

Teacher instructions Su 3, 3

Solve the addition calculations on each rocket. First add 10 and write the answer on each planet. Then take away 1 and write the answer on each moon.

Date ____________

Addition addresses

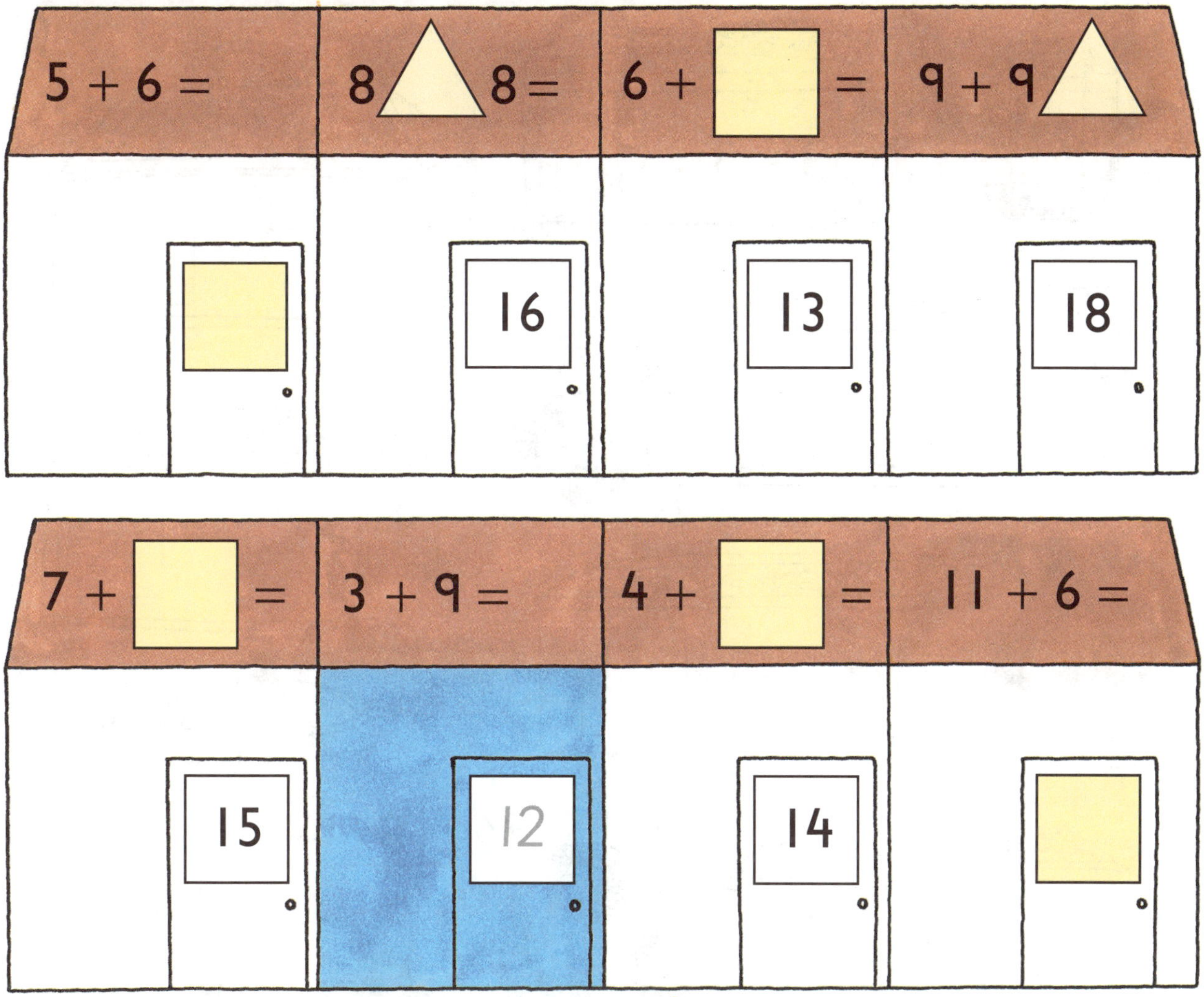

Teacher instructions Su 3, 4

Find the missing number or symbol to complete each addition sum. Write it in the space. Then colour the house to match the number or symbol on the T-shirt.

Date ______________

Treasure addition

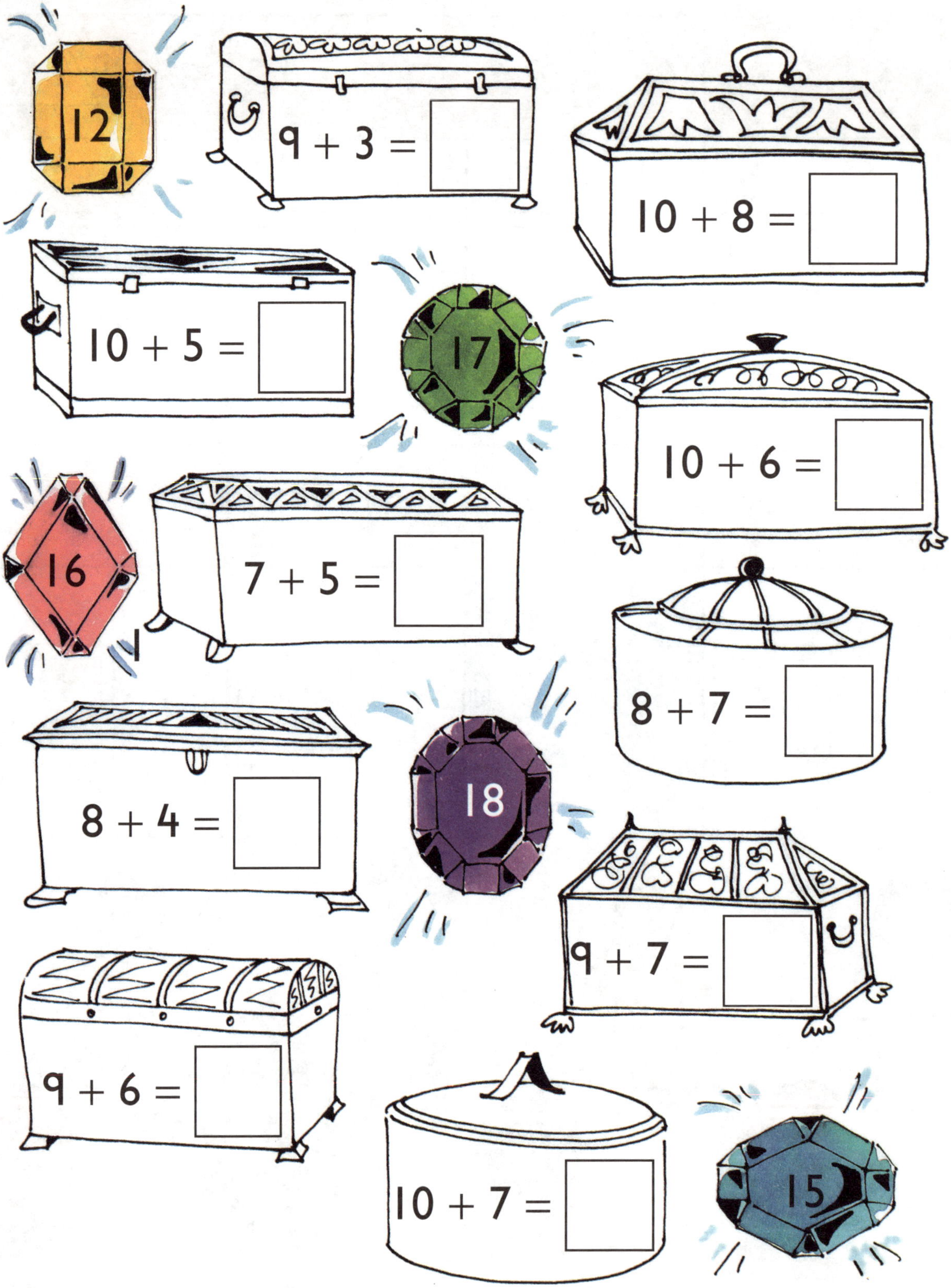

Teacher instructions Su 3, 5
Solve the addition problem on each treasure chest then colour the chest to match the jewel showing the correct total.

Date ____________

Subtraction rescue

Teacher instructions Su 4, 1

Look at the subtraction calculation on each tower. Then colour its flag and turret to match the shield showing the correct total.

Date ____________

Subtraction facts

16 − 5 = ☐

18 − 6 = ☐

17 − 3 = ☐

19 − 4 = ☐

17 − ☐ = 14

19 − ☐ = 15

16 − ☐ = 11

18 − ☐ = 12

☐ − 5 = 11

☐ − 3 = 14

☐ − 4 = 15

☐ − 6 = 12

Teacher instructions Su 4, 2

Find the missing number in each of the subtraction calculations and write it in the empty box.

Date ______________

Shopping sums

Which coins would you use?

rubber and pencil 1p + 2p + 5p

highlight and rubber ______________

pencil and felt tip ______________

two pencils ______________

two rubbers ______________

two rubbers and a pencil ______________

What is your change from 20p?

ruler ______________

sharpener ______________

pencil ______________

rubber and highlight ______________

two rubbers ______________

rubber and a pencil ______________

Teacher instructions Su 4, 3
Look at the picture. Work out which coins you will need to pay for the items. Now calculate your change from 20p.

Date ______________

How much is the yoyo?

3p	6p	7p	5p

Teacher instructions Su 4, 4

In each picture, write the price of the yoyo in the space above it. Then colour in the coins which are needed to buy the yoyo.

Date ______________

Pizza toppings

	Total	Change from 20p
	12p	

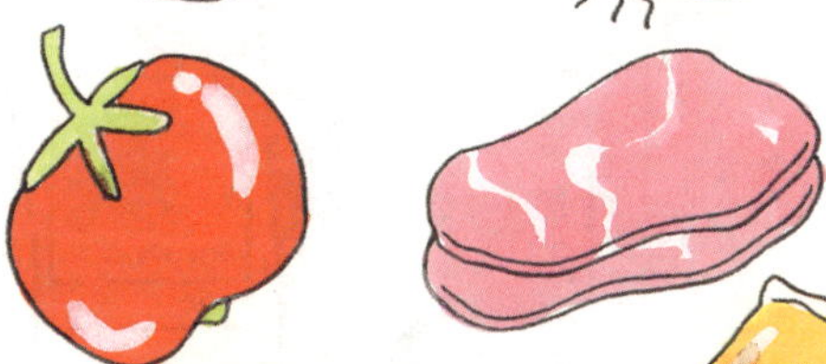		

Teacher instructions Su 4, 5

In each row, work out the cost of the pizza toppings and the change you will get from 20p. Write the answers in the spaces provided.

Date ____________

Topsy-turvy 2s

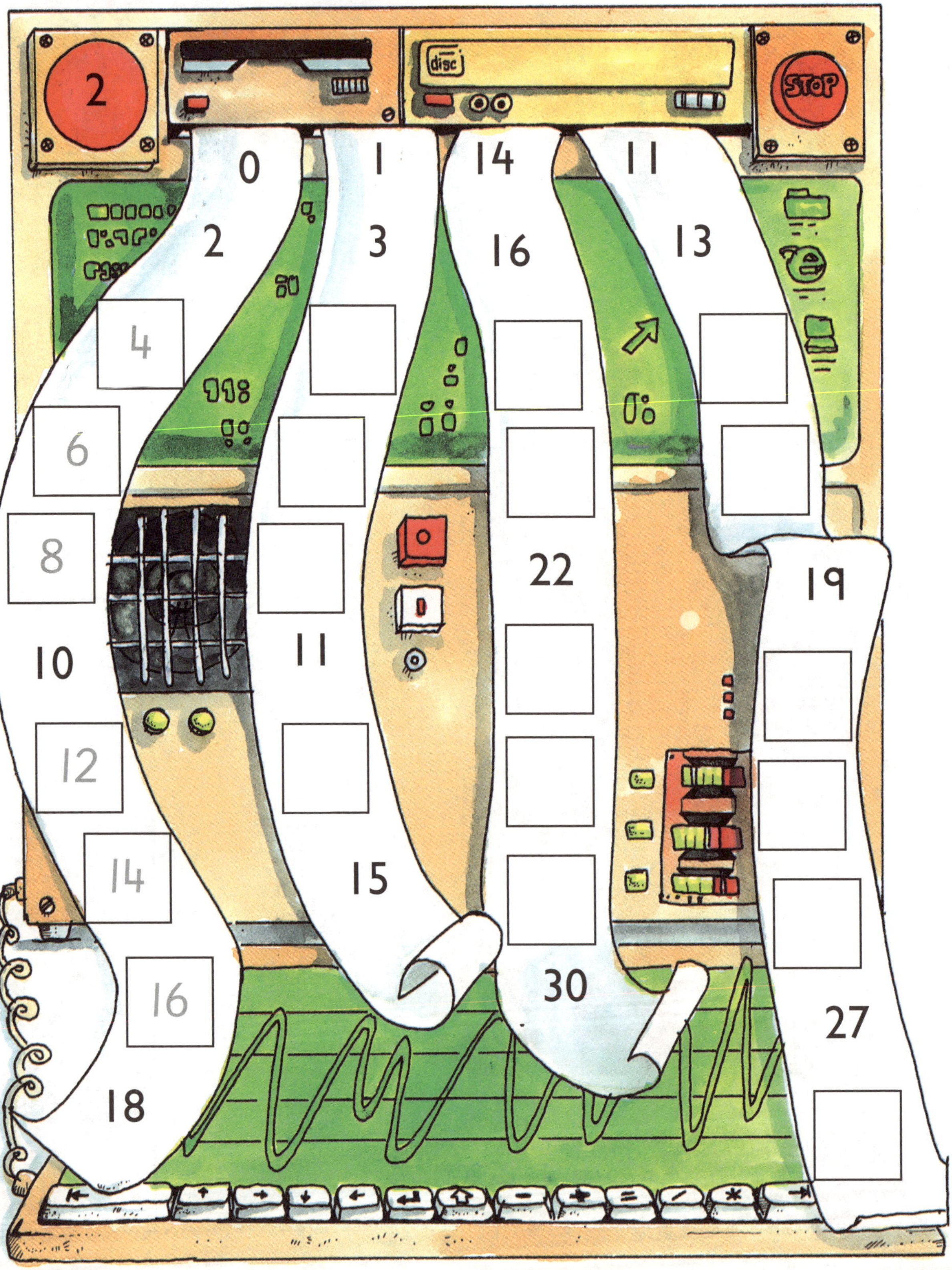

Teacher instructions Su 7, 1

Look at each computer print-out and decide whether it was counting in 2s from 0 or 1. Then write in the missing numbers.

Date ________

Odds and Evens Farm

Teacher instructions Su 7, 2
Count each group of animals. Write the number in red if it is odd and blue if it is even.

Date ____________

Furball 5s and troll 3s

Teacher instructions Su 7, 3

Look at the numbers at the side and use them to complete each sequence, counting in 3s or 5s. Colour each number when you have used it.

Date ______________

Exploring planet 9

Teacher instructions Su 7, 4
Trace the route of each alien to its spaceship and find the number which, when added to the alien, makes a total of 9. Write this number on the spaceship.

Date ____________

Chilly problems

5 + 5 + 5 = 15

☐ + ☐ + ☐ = 15

☐ + ☐ + ☐ = 15

☐ + ☐ + ☐ = 15

☐ + ☐ + ☐ = 15

Teacher instructions Su 7, 5

In each row, write three numbers which, when added together, make 15. Use the penguins to help you.

Date ____________

Confused counting machines

Teacher instructions Su 8, 1

In each row, colour the 2 numbers which are in the wrong order.
Now write the numbers underneath, this time in the right order.

Date ____________

Guessing gorilla

Teacher instructions Su 8, 2

Quickly look at the bananas in each picture then cover it with your hand. Write your estimate in the top space. Now count each banana and write the number underneath.

Date ____________

Clothes estimate

There are ☐ caps.

There are ☐ shorts.

There are ☐ vests.

There are ☐ jumpers.

Teacher instructions Su 8, 3

Quickly look at the clothes in each picture then cover it with your hand. Write your estimate in the top space. Now count each piece of clothing and write the number underneath.

Date ____________

Doubles to the Ark

 1 +  1 = 2

 □ +  □ = □

 □ +  □ = □

 □ +  □ = □

 □ +  □ = □

Teacher instructions Su 8, 4

In each row, draw the missing parts on the second animal so that it matches its double. Count the parts on each animal and write the numbers in the boxes. Complete the calculation.

Begin to know addition and subtraction facts … to at least 10

Date ____________

Pirate addition and subtraction

Teacher instructions Su 8, 5

Solve the addition and subtraction problems on each ship and then colour the ship to match the island showing the correct total.

Date ____________

Big Foot

6 + ◯ = 10

7 + ◯ = 9

◯ − 6 = 3

◯ − 4 = 4

6 − ◯ = 2

◯ + 8 = 10

10 − ◯ = 3

◯ + 3 = 7

Teacher instructions Su 9, 1

All the sums were correct before Big Foot the gorilla stepped all over the page. The missing parts of the sums need to be worked out again. Write the correct numbers in the circles.

Date ____________

Adding to 10 and 20

10 + 6 = ☐

20 + 3 = ☐

10 + 4 = ☐

20 + 7 = ☐

10 + 3 = ☐

Teacher instructions Su 9, 2

Count the fingers and thumbs on each child and write the number in the box on their shirt. Find the calculation which matches each pair or group of children. Shade their shirts the same colour.

Date ____________

Subtracting from 10 and 20

10 – 3 = ___

10 – ___ = ___

10 – ___ = ___

20 – ___ = ___

20 – ___ = ___

20 – ___ = ___

Teacher instructions Su 9, 2

Count the fingers and thumbs on each child. Follow the instruction to hide some fingers by crossing them out. Then write the subtraction calculation underneath.

Date ____________

Tens and Units take off!

11 + 12 = 23

□ + □ = □

□ + □ = □

□ + □ = □

Teacher instructions Su 9, 3

In each panel, look at the number of tens and units on each planet. Colour the total number in the spaceship. Write the tens and units in the boxes in the spaceship. Then complete the addition calculation.

Date ____________

Tens and Units take off!

☐ + ☐ = ☐

☐ + ☐ = ☐

☐ + ☐ = ☐

☐ + ☐ = ☐

Teacher instructions Su 9, 3

In each panel, look at the number of tens and units on each planet. Colour the total number in the spaceship. Write the tens and units in the boxes in the spaceship. Then complete the addition calculation.

Date ____________

Anemone addition

3 + 10 = 13

3 + ___ = 13

___ + 10 = 13

5 + 10 = ___

5 + ___ = 15

___ + 10 = 15

6 + 10 = ___

6 + ___ = 16

___ + 10 = 16

8 + 10 = ___

8 + ___ = 18

___ + 10 = 18

Teacher instructions Su 9, 4

In each panel, look at the addition problems. Work out which flower shows the missing number for each. Write the missing number in each calculation and colour the flower to match.

Date ____________

Sunflower subtraction

3 13 10

13 − 10 =

13 − = 3

− 10 = 3

14 4 10

14 − 10 =

14 − = 4

− 10 = 4

10 7 17

17 − 10 =

17 − = 7

− 10 = 7

10 19 9

19 − 10 =

19 − = 9

− 10 = 9

Teacher instructions Su 9, 4

In each panel, look at the subtraction problems. Work out which flower shows the missing number for each. Write the missing number in each calculation and colour the flower to match.

Date ____________

Bridging through 10

7 + 6 = ☐

8 + 4 = ☐

9 + 5 = ☐

3 + 8 = ☐

4 + 9 = ☐

5 + 8 = ☐

6 + 9 = ☐

7 + 4 = ☐

5 + 6 = ☐

Teacher instructions Su 9, 5

Solve the addition calculations by bridging through 10.

Bridge in the jungle

16 + 8 = ☐

18 + 5 = ☐

17 + 6 = ☐

12 + 9 = ☐

14 + 7 = ☐

15 + 8 = ☐

9 + 13 = ☐

6 + 19 = ☐

17 + 5 = ☐

7 + 16 = ☐

4 + 18 = ☐

Teacher instructions Su 10, 1

Solve the addition calculations by bridging through 20.

Bridging through 20

13 + 7 = 20 + 1 = 21

☐ + ☐ = 20 + ☐ = ☐

☐ + ☐ = ☐ + ☐ = ☐

☐ + ☐ = ☐ + ☐ = ☐

Teacher instructions Su 10, 2

Bridge to 20 by counting the steps to the bridge and from the bridge to the castle. Write out your calculation in the spaces underneath. Write the total in the crown.

Date ____________

Fairground problems

9 people were on the dodgems. 6 more people joined them.

How many were left on the dodgems?

9 + 6 = 15

18 people were on the rollercoaster. Tom, Amir and Ellis got off.

How many were left on the rollercoaster?

There were 20 toffee apples. Emma bought 1 of them.

How many toffee apples were left?

There were 11 prizes on the top shelf. There were 7 more on the bottom shelf.

How many prizes altogether?

Teacher instructions Su 10, 3
Read each number problem. Then write the addition or subtraction calculation in the spaces provided.

Date ____________

Adding up the menu

MENU

pizza 10p

chicken curry 11p

beans 18p

milk 7p

veggie burger 8p

chips 9p

patty 12p

juice 4p

Hattie spends

10 + 9 = 19

Hattie's change is

20 – 19 = ☐

Cavan spends

☐ + ☐ = ☐

Cavan's change is

20 – ☐ = ☐

Tom spends

☐ + ☐ = ☐

Tom's change is

20 – ☐ = ☐

Yuko spends

☐ + ☐ = ☐

Yuko's change is

20 – ☐ = ☐

Teacher instructions Su 10, 4

Look at the menu. Each child has 20p. First work out how much each child spends. Then calculate the change each child receives.

Date ____________

Seaside problems

Samir and Gita have 2 fishing nets.

Suzi has 1 fishing net.
How many fishing nets do they have?

☐ + ☐ = ☐

The children have 9 sandwiches.

They give 2 to a bird.
How many sandwiches are left?

☐ − ☐ = ☐

Samir has 11 seashells in his net.

Suzi has 6.
How many seashells do they have?

☐ + ☐ = ☐

The children made 13 sandcastles.

The sea washed away 5.
How many sandcastles are left?

☐ − ☐ = ☐

Teacher instructions Su 10, 5
Read each number problem. Then write the addition or subtraction calculation in the spaces provided.

Counting leaves

☐ branches have 2 leaves.

☐ branches have 5 leaves.

☐ branches have 1 leaf.

Teacher instructions Su 12, 2
Count the leaves on each branch. Draw a leaf in the correct column to represent each branch. Then complete the sentences.

Date ____________

Sorting letters ...

1, 1, 1, ____

Teacher instructions Su 12, 3

Cross off a letter. Write its number on the correct door. Then write the numbers on the line from the smallest to largest.

Date ______________

… and parcels

1, 1, 1,

Teacher instructions Su 12, 3

Cross off a parcel. Write its number in the correct sack. Then write the numbers on the line from the smallest to largest.

Date ______________

Fish or flower?

Colour

The first colour is ☐.

The last colour is ☐.

The second colour is ☐.

fish	
flower	

Colour	Number
blue	
yellow	

There are ☐ fish.

There are ☐ flowers.

Teacher instructions Su 12, 4

Place a counter on a fish. Roll a die and move the counter. Write the colour in the list. Draw a fish or flower in the table at the bottom. Complete the sentences.

 Date ____________

Letter train

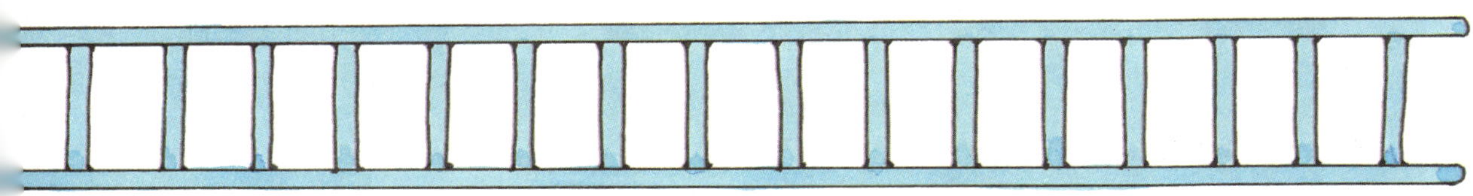

Letter	Number
A	
B	
C	
D	

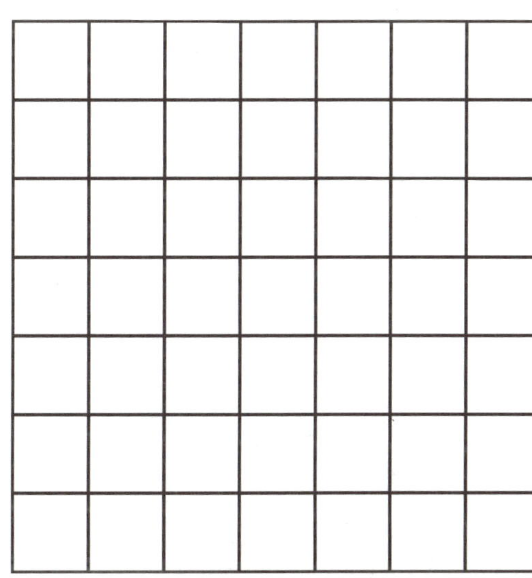

Teacher instructions Su 12, 5
Cross off each letter. Write it on the correct train carriage. Then write all the letters in alphabetical order on the track. Complete the table and colour a square for each letter.

Collins Primary Maths is specifically written to The Framework for Teaching Mathematics. The course provides daily maths lessons for each school year running from Reception/Foundation Stage to Year 6, and is matched to the relevant Scottish 5-14 Programme for P1 to P7. Through its comprehensive teacher and pupil material, **Collins Primary Maths** supports teachers in achieving high levels of numeracy with their whole class.

Number Workbook 3 provides pupil practice of Number objectives covered in the Summer term of Year 1. Each page is linked to a lesson plan in the **Collins Primary Maths Teacher's Guide**, and the work provides pupil consolidation which flows directly from the main teaching activity.

Other Workbooks in **Collins Primary Maths**

Number Workbook 1, covering Autumn term work	000 315262 6
Number Workbook 2, covering Spring term work	000 315263 4
Measures, Shape and Space Workbook, covering the year	000 315265 0

Published by Collins Educational
An imprint of HarperCollins Publishers Ltd
77-85 Fulham Palace Road
Hammersmith
London W6 8JB
www.fireandwater.com

First published 1999
Reprinted 2000

ISBN 0 00 315264 2

Printed by Scotprint

ISBN 0-00-315264-2

9 780003 152647 >